r father
n hvn

Simon Jenkins is the editor of ship-of-fools.com, the acclaimed online community and 'magazine of Christian unrest', which is currently attracting over 1 million page views per month from visitors chiefly in the UK and USA. Simon is also an independent writer and designer. His previous books include *The Bible From Scratch*, *Windows into Heaven* and *The Bible Map Book*.

r father
n hvn

written and edited by
Simon Jenkins

Westminster John Knox Press
LOUISVILLE • LONDON

© 2002 ship-of-fools.com

Book design by ship-of-fools.biz
Cover design by ship-of-fools.biz
Cover illustration: Simon Jenkins

First edition
Published by Westminster John Knox Press
Louisville, Kentucky

Printed and bound in Great Britain by The Cromwell Press, Wiltshire

02 03 04 05 06 07 08 09 10 11 — 10 9 8 7 6 5 4 3 2 1

Library of Congress Cataloging-in-Publication Data is on file at the Library of Congress, Washington, D.C.

A catalogue record for this book is available from the British Library

ISBN 0 664 22598 5

contnts

nu testmnt

intro

This book started out as a competition on ship-of-fools.com, the UK online magazine of Christian unrest.

We wanted to see who could write the smartest version of the Lord's Prayer in a single txt msg. This meant reducing the 372 characters of the traditional prayer down to just 160 characters, without losing anything important.

The prayers people sent in began, 'R boss,' 'dad@heaven,' and even 'yo G', and the winning prayer ended, '4 eva! ok?' They were funny, inventive and even prayable. You can find some of them on page 119.

So here's a book that casts the net wider than Jesus' prayer. This too is from a competition on ship-of-fools.com, where we asked our shipmates to send us their most-enjoyed bits of the Bible, boiled down to the size of a txt msg.

It's an intriguing process, because it's not just about squeezing verses to fit onto the small screen, but getting to the heart of what you think the Good Book is saying. And then putting it into the language of now.

Seeing how people have done this is an entertainment in itself. But hopefully the texts in this book will become real txts, too, sent from person to person, freeing the words of the Bible from the printed page and making them live.

d bay6

dictionry

Here's a list of most of the shortcuts used in this book. We haven't included the standard abbreviations (e.g. IMO = In My Opinion). Instead, we've gone for strings that mostly explain themselves.

@	at
£££	money
$$$	money
%	oo (f%l = fool)
&	and
*	star
?s	questions
÷	divide
1der	wonder
10der	tender
10shun	tension

2day	today
2morra	tomorrow
24/7	all the time (24 hours a day, 7 days a week)
4bid	forbid
4biddn	forbidden
4C	foresee
4father	forefather
4get	forget
4giv	forgive
4midable	formidable
4nic8	fornicate
4sake	forsake
4skin	foreskin
4tnite	fortnight
4tress	fortress
4tune	fortune
4ward	forward

a10shun	attention
B	be
B4	before
B9	benign
bay6	basics
C	see / sea
complic8d	complicated
cre8	create

D-b8	debate
d8	date
desecr8	desecrate
EZ	easy
EZ-PZ	easy-peasy
f8	fate
FR	ever
G!	gee!
g8	gate
H2O	water
K9	canine
K?	OK?
L8	late
M4sis	emphasis
M4size	emphasise

m8	mate
MT	empty
n	and
NE	any
NE1	anyone
NEbody	anybody
NJL	angel
NME	enemy
NRG	energy
NT	New Testament
NV	envy
of10	often
OT	Old Testament
phy6	physics
pil8	Pilate
pl8	plate
po10t	potent
Q	question

R	are, our
r8	rate
re5al	revival
rel8	relate
RMe	army
S8n	Satan
st8	state
str8	straight
sur5al	survival
ta2	tattoo
tr8tor	traitor
tx	thanks
U	you
v	very
w/	with
w8	wait

x	kiss
Xn	Christian
Xt	Christ
Y?	why?
z	is
zzz	sleep / snoring

d nu
hieroglyphix

Writing started out as pictures (Egypt at
the time of Moses used pictograms) so
the way emoticons are used in text
messages and email is a real throwback.
Here are some handy hieroglyphics for
the sanctified cellphone.

useful symbols

0:-)	Angel
X0:-)	Fallen angel
0:-*	Holy kiss
}:-*	Unholy kiss
:-P	Sticking your tongue out
:-PPPP	Speaking in tongues

<><	Fish
<ICHTHUS><	Ichthus fish
<JESUS><	Jesus fish
<):-(><	Jonah inside fish
3:-{#>	The Evil One
3B-{#>	The Evil One partying in Ibiza
3:-{#> 3--oo--	The Evil One (holding a trident)
U/-\~	Bull
:-@	Cursing
:-@%*$	Parental advisory cursing
%-)	Drunk
\o/	Hallelujah!
<3	Heart
-|--(	Calvary
+ T +	Calvary (horizontal)
~===	Candle
+-	Little cross

>+	Cross on a chain
}	Spirit descends as a dove
}%	Dove brings olive branch to Noah
+<::|	Church
<::|	Synagogue
|::>+	Church of Satan
0-+	Female
0->	Male

biblical cast (in order of appearance)

000I:-###	God
(:-) : 8-	Adam
(:-) 3 >-	Eve
II	Lot's wife
IIIIIIIIII o-|--<	Jacob (ladder to heaven)
//oo\\	Samson (pre-haircut)
@:-) 3	Delilah

20

]:-)	King David
]:-) §–8-<	David dancing before the Lord
]:$)	King Solomon
(8^::	Job (covered in boils)
:.-(	Jeremiah
]:-1####	King Nebchadnezzar
0(:-) 8	Virgin Mary
0(:-) 8 (@)-	Mary expecting
0~:)	Baby Jesus
]:-(<=oo=	King Herod (holding spear)
0(:-{)}	Jesus (happy)
0(:-{)} (--|=	Jesus (full length)
0):-{(}	Jesus (angry)
&:-)##	St Peter
%^{...	Gadarene demoniac
E:8)	Gadarene swine (pre-plunge)

`((():-(`	High priest Caiaphas
`0):-(##`	St Paul
`(:-)33333|--<`	Diana, goddess of the Ephesians

characters

`+{{{:-)`	Pope
`+{{{:-)(-||-|=`	Full-length Pope
`+C|:-) >-+`	Orthodox bishop
`<+(:-) >-+`	Catholic bishop
`{[:-) ~=oo=`	Anglo-Catholic (carrying candle)
`(:-) >+`	Monk
`[(:-) >+`	Nun
`:-D >+`	Charismatic
`):-(`	Calvinist
`c):-(`	N. Ireland Protestant
`d:-p >+`	Youth worker

:-V >+	Preacher
$:-) ></// >	Televangelist
<|):-(<--	Puritan
(:-0)$	Choirboy
_0_ _0_ _0_	Church choir
\0/ \0/ \0/	Gospel choir
:-/ >+	Sceptical believer

How Methuselah got to be so old.

`*<I:-)##`	Santa Claus
`<):-( {__`	Grim reaper

saints, etc.

`(:-)=====I`	St Simon Stylites
`(-: 33`	St Francis (with birds)
`(:-1))`	Martin Luther
`:-( +- Σ`	John Wesley after
	nine hours on a horse
`( :-?`	C.S. Lewis (with pipe)
`0//:-) >+`	Mother Teresa
`3..(:-1)`	Martin Luther King Jr.
	(having a dream)
`B-D >+`	Desmond Tutu
`@:-D >+`	Born-again Elvis
`&:-&)&&`	Philip Yancey
`8^#) >+`	Ned Flanders
`( 8^(1) >+`	Homer gets religion

seven deadly sins

:^)))	Pride
(:o)000	Gluttony
):-) : ^	Lust
)8^(	Envy
(3-I)	Sloth
~):-0	Anger
):-P...	Covetousness

round d Bble in 58 txts

Some people spend years locked inside theology seminaries trying to learn about the Bible. But now, you can become an instant Bible bore with this rapid rundown of all the books in the Good Book. Each of the following messages contains 160 characters or less (excluding the titles).

genesis

God cre8s hvn&erth. Adam&Eve givn XLent garden. Eve 8 appl & all goes pear-shapd. 1st murder & big flud follo. But Abe, Zak, Jake & Joe Bcum Gods chosen ppl...

exodus

Gods ppl R slaves in Egypt. Moses: "Let my ppl go!" Fairo: "RU joking?" 10 plagues L8r & ppl set free. They go2 desert. Eat manna. Get 10 comandts. &break em...

leviticus

"Dnt h8 yr bro, dnt marry yr sis, luv yr naybr. Wanna eat pigs or b@s? 4get it! BarBQ bulls 4God. Respect old ppl. No ta2s! B holy coz im holy," sez God.

numbers

Moses sez 2 ppl: "Ill lead U2 d land of milk&huny!" But ppl not imprest &moan @him. God's vext: "OK, stay in d dezut 4 40ys, til evry1 of U dies!" So it hapens.

deuteronomy

Wan2 hear Moses gr8est hits? This=them. 4 big speeches in d dezut &then Big Mo dies. "Hear Israel, dLord RGod is 1. Luv him 24/7 w/all Uhave." Th@s his msg.

joshua

Getting in2 land of K-nan not EZ. Josh knu how 2do it. Xd Riva Jordn, @ackd cities, dmolishd walls oJeriko, 1 big b@les, conqrd ppl. Lotsa bl%d, deth&horra.

judges

Israel's NMEs hit back but d Judges (Gideon, Samson, Deborah, etc.) cum 2da resQ. If U like grilla warfare &tit4tat revenge, this bk is 4U. V.Dpressing.

ruth

Ruth (gentile grl) weds Jewish boy who L8r dies. Then her mum-n-law's widowd 2. Ruth stix w/her &sez "yr God willB my God." Ruth Bcums KgDavid's gr8-granma.

1 samuel

Sam: "Saul, UBcum king, OK?" Saul: "Thanx!" L8R, Sam has 2nd thorts. Sam: "David, UBcum king insted, OK?" Dave: "C%l!" Now there R2 kings in 1 land. Duh!

2 samuel

KgDavid Cs sexy grl on nxt-d%r r%f. Tries ch@-up line: "Im hot4U". "&me4U" she sez. S%n she's preg &Dave has her hubby killd 2coverup. Then uvas start 2die...

1 kings

He's Yz. Has fame&4tune. &700wives. Yes... its KgSolomon. He bilds temple 4God. His kingdm's ÷d in 2 when he dies. &lotsa kings (g%d &bad) follo him.

2 kings

This bk goes from king2king2king... til the RMe of Babylon breaks in2 Jeruslm, desecr8s temple &4ces the ppl in2 Xile. Itsa terribl f8 & l%ks like The End.

1&2 chronicles

Wan2 read the story of KingDave but w/out d naughty bits? Me neither. These bks rel8 almost the same story as 1&2Kings but w/ less ova rock'n'roll M4sis.

ezra

Afta 70ys in Xile... joy! The J%ish ppl R sent home &rebild KgSolomon's temple. 100 bulls &400 lambs R barBQd @ d big opening bash.

nehemiah

Nehemiah's in a st8. Jeruslm's a ruin &he's desper8 2rebild it. Da Persian King givs him d OK. But there R big 10shuns coz his NMEs try 2stop him...

esther

Xerxes (Persian King) wants nu wife. Esther (Jewish stunna)=prrfect. Haman (King's favrite) plans 2kill all Jews in d Persian Mpire. Queen Esther 2da resQ!

job

Job's blessed: 10kids, 3k camels, 7k sheep &lotsa $$$. But God takes his g%d 4tune away. "Y, oh Y?" asx Job. Lots more ?s & d-b8 follo: Y do g%d ppl suffa?

psalms

Welcum 2da Bbles m%diest bk. 1 minit its
up nHevn & d next its down in d dudu.
God's prayzd, sins R fessed & joy'n'gloom
Xprest. Its human&divine all in 1.

proverbs

Wan2B Yz? Wan2put yr life on d str8
&narro? Wan2get yr feet on d rt Rd? Here R
100s of sayings&riddles so th@ NE1 can
lern d bay6 of how 2B Yz &not a f%l.

ecclesiastes

Mr Ecclesiastes l%x round &dspairs @
evrythng he Cs. Suxess, $$$, lafter, wine,
women etc. all leave him MT, coz evry1
meets d same f8. We all die & th@s th@.

song of songs

Him: Yr eyes Rlike doves. Her: &yr legs Rlike pillas of marbl. Him: &yr bzms Rlike gazelles. Her: &yr... hang on... bzms like gazelles?? Him: yeah. Wanna d8?

isaiah

God hada tuf msg 4 d ppl of Jruslem but cudnt find NE1 to Dliver it. "Who'll go 4us?" he askd. "I will!" sed Isaiah. &thats how Izzy Bcame Gods own txt msg.

jeremiah

Jerry woz a profit. He cd 4C d future &it was all gl%m & d%m. "Turn back 2 God B4 its 2 L8!" he sed. But his NMEs thru him in a pit &calld him a tr8tor.

lamentations

This bk's a weepie. Cryin, weepin, sobbin, moanin'n'groanin... its gottem all. Fair enuf, tho. Jeruslm had bn conqd & d ppl takn in2 Xile. Bring yr own hanky.

ezekiel

Zeke: livd in Bbylon w/da J%ish Xiles. Saw visions. Had uniq way of preachng: shavd his head, 8 a b%k, lay on his side 4a year. Seriusly weird (in a c%l way).

daniel

Dan=da worlds 1st lion-tamer. Was also gr8 @ rel8ting d meaning of d'Kings rt royl nitemares. 4 all this he Bcame a VIP in Bbylon w/a 70yr career as a profit.

hosea

H. wuz in luv. Got maryd. But his wyf cheatd on im. "Me 2," sed God. "I luvd Israel &she left me." H. 4gave his wyf, x-ed &made up. &so did God w/Israel.

joel

Dis bk's got 1000s & 1000s of insex... crEpy-crawly locusts wich 8 evrythng in site. "Put yr life str8," sez Joel, "B4 God sends d locusts 4U2!"

amos

Israel had loadsa $$$. But while d VIPs livd in luxry, wiv jools &wine &slaves, d poor cd barely sur5. Amos @ackd d rich &told em 2B just. A bk 4 2day, then.

obadiah

Da shortest bk in d OT (jus 21 verses) is also v.short-tempud. Obie cusses d Edomites (d Israelites' cuzuns) &sez theyll B dstroyd. Yes, it's payback time...

jonah

Jonah woz suposd 2go2 Nineveh (a wickd city) but ran awa insted, got thrown in2 da C & ended up in d wrong plaice. Yes... it's d Bble meets Jaws.

Jonah tries to get a signal.

micah

Recognize dis? "They wil beat their swords in2 plowshares..." Or dis? "Act justly, luv mercy &wlk humbly w/yr Gd." Both by our boy, Micah. He's world-famus.

nahum & habakkuk

Wot do Uwant 1st? Da g%d news (Nahum) or d bad news (Haba)? G%d: d evil Asyrian Mpire's been conqd! Bad: d even mo evil Bbylonian Mpire's taken ovr. Gl%m.

zephaniah

@10shun! Stand wel bak! Zeph=a small bk, but its Xplosive! It 4Cs d end of d world: Gods v.(x1000) angry & dstroys evrythng w/fire. So... repent PDQ!

haggai, zechariah & malachi

Hag, Zak & Mal gave their msgs afta d J%z had cum home frm Xile. Zak's famus words (500 ys B4 Gzus): "Yr king cums 2U, humble &riding on a donkey..."

matthew

Da 3 kings follo da *. D Holy Babe goes 2Egypt. Gzus tels d parabl of d 10 virgns. Judas hangs hiself. Soljus gard Gzus' t%m. U wont find these bits anywer els.

mark

Mark Cs Gzus as Axion Man. Healng, preachng, xorcizng, ch%sing his m8s - all cum @ a fast&furious r8. Gzus walks on H2O &breaks d laws of phy6. Kpow!

luke

Luke had an I 4 da ladies. &also 4 d poor, lepers, imigrants &uva hated ppl. In Luke, Gzus givs em all speshl respect. "Da 1st wilB last & d last 1st," he sez.

john

God luvd dworld so gr8ly he sent his 1&only son, so NE1 who blievs in him wil liv 4eva &not die. Th@s Johns msg on a pl8. Gzus=da way home 2God.

acts

Acts= the Cquel 2 Luke. Gzus ascends 2hvn. Da chrch is cre8d when d Sprit falls. Da believas R perCQted. & StPaul gets convertd &Bcums d brains Bhind d nu faif.

romans

Paul: Evry1 has sind & is an NME of God.
There4 evry1 should die coz d wages of
sin=death. But God sends Gzus 2die in R
place. He makes us @1 w/God. QED.

1&2 corinthians

Corinth = d Las Vegas of d 1st century &da
church had lotsa 10shuns w/b%ze, sex,
laws%ts, etc. They were v. ÷d. Paul rote &
told em: "Luv is da gr8est."

galatians

1 of d big D-b8s 4 d 1st blievas was: "do I
hav2 Bcum a J% B4 I can Bcum a Xn?" Paul
sez: "No! Yr not livin unda d old law" &
adds: "Oi! Keep yr 4skins on!"

ephesians

Wan2C d big pikcha? By grace Uve bin savd.
UR a citizn of hvn. Wan2 hav down-2-erf
advce 4 livng z God ment U2? 4giv uvas.
Dont 4nic8. Liv as a child of d lite.

philippians

Paul's in prisn, on trial 4his life. But he
sends a letta 2 1of his fave chrches: Filipi.
Its 10der & persnal, telling them 2 "shine
like *s" in v.dark times.

colossians

Gzus... who is he? This letta=where 2 l%k 4
da answer. "He's d image of d invisible
God," sez Paul, "d 1stborn of creation, &
evrythng was cr8d by & 4 him..."

1&2 thessalonians

He'll return w/out warning, like a thief @nite. & he'll cum w/fire &trumpets &powrful angels 2 overthrow S8n. Paul Dscribes d return of Gzus @ d end of time.

1 timothy

Tim was Paul's RH man, altho he was a bit ova wimp. Here, Paul gr%ms Tim 2Bcum his suxessor, even nagging him "2drink a litl wine 2 calm yr stomach". P%r Tim!

2 timothy

Rome: Paul W8s in prisn 2B XEQtd. This=his last-eva letta & he writes his own epitaf: "I hav fort d g%d fite, I hav finishd d race, I hav kept d faif..."

titus

Titus=a man w/a mission. Paul left him on Crete 2 l%k afta d nu churches. But d uva chrch leadas didn respect Titus. So Paul sent in d rein4cments: this letta!

philemon

1ce upon a time there was a slave calld "Useful" who turnd out 2B useless &ran awa. He met Paul &Bcam a Xn. Paul sent him bak 2his owner, carryng this letta...

hebrews

Complic8d bk, this 1! Ina nutshell: Gzus = gr8er than hi-priests &Moses. His bl%ds betta than d bl%d of OT sacrifces. Gzus knox the OT 4 6 &opens a nu way 2God.

james

James ("call me Jim") h8s the EZ-PZ sorta faith. He wants it 2B tuf, costly &real. "Faith w/out axion is ded" he sez. Its not gd enuf 2say U blieve. Just do it.

1 peter

Pete writes 2 prep Gods ppl 4 perCQshun by d Roman st8. He tels em 2live good lives B4 the pagans &he points2 d suffring of Gzus as their e.g. &inspiration.

2 peter

Y the delay, then? Y hasnt Gzus cum bak, as he promisd? Y,OY? "Bcoz God is patient" sez this letta. He'll cum bak OK, but givs ppl time 2turn 2him B4 its 2 L8.

1,2&3 john

3 littl lettas filld w/deep&wide ideas. "God is luv... God is lite &in him is no darknss @ all... If we confess R sins he wil 4giv... we must luv 1 anuva."

jude

Last-but-1 bk of d Bble. Bite-sizd. Writn 2 @ack heretix in d church. &Jude really goes 4 it: "Woe 2them!" he sez, "those wild beasts &wandring *s." Hey, Jude!

revelation

Da Bble's big ending, wiv a cast of 1000s: d hor of Bbylon, 4 riders of d apoclypse, d gr8 S8n. &above all, d Kg of Kgs &Lord of Lords, who wipes awa evry tear.

d dead C txts

A major archeological find was made in 1999. A used car salesman, on holiday near the Dead Sea, heard a phone trilling in a cave in some ancient cliffs and found the long sought-after Nokia 1800BC cellphone. On it were stored many txt msgs sent in Bible times, all in picture form. Your task, should you accept it, is to decipher them. Answers can be found on page 139.

1.   B^(---> 8^)

2.   E:8) x1000 ---> H2O

3.   ]:-)]:-)]:-) —> *

4.   ]:$) .... :=81

5.   &(:-)## ----<o><

6.   ):-(### o---- ---> ~~~~o<

7.   <>(:-) ---> (:-P

8.   _i_/ ---> >< i >

9.   #(:-)## ---> 8>< ---> (:-(

10.   00000 <>< <><

11.   _____iiiiii_____/////

12.   /////eeeee\\\\\

txt blessings

When was the last time you blessed someone? When they sneezed, probably. The Bible is full of blessings, which either means people sneezed a lot in those days, or that blessings were a bigger deal then than now. Here's the pick of blessings used by Paul, David and others...

May d Lord of peace hiself givU wall2wall peace 24/7.
2 Thessalonians 3:16

May U grasp how wide &long &hi &deep is d luv of Xt, &kno dis luv dats biggr &betta than NEthing els.
Ephesians 3:18-19

May d Lord ansa U when UR in distress.
Psalm 20:1

May d God of hope fil U w/all joy &peace in
blievng so th@ hope flows from U to uvas
in d powr of d Sprit.
Romans 15:13

May d grace of d Lord Gzus, & d luv of God,
& d compny of d Holy Sprit, B w/us all.
2 Corinthians 13:14

May d Lord make R luv 4 each uva go up&up
til it overflows.
1 Thessalonians 3:12

May God B good 2U&me both. &may he
bless us &let us liv in the lite of his face.
Psalm 67:1

May UB fild 2 d top w/all d fulness of God.
Ephesians 3:19

May d God of peace make U holy thruNthru.
May da whole of U - spirit, soul&body - B
kept 100% clean @ d return of R Lord Gzus.
1 Thessalonians 5:23

May d Lord yr God B with U.
2 Samuel 14:17

May d Lord blessU &keepU. May d Lord shine
his face onU &B grashus 2U. May d Lord
turn his face 2ward U &giv U peace.
Numbers 6:24-26

May he make U strong w/his Sprit's powr in yr
inna being, so tht Xt livs in yr hart thru faith.
Ephesians 3:16-17

May UB blessed when U cum home &blessed when U go awa.
Deuteronomy 28:6

May d Lord yr God bless U in all d work of yr hands.
Deuteronomy 14:29

May he make R hearts strong so th@ we'll B blameless &holy in d presnce of R God & Fatha when R Lord Gzus returns w/all his holy 1s.
1 Thessalonians 3:13

May d God of peace, who brort R Lord Gzus back from d dead (th@ gr8 shepherd of d sheep) equip U w/evrythng good 4 doing his wil.
Hebrews 13:20-21

Lord, may yr blessing B on yr ppl.
Psalm 3:8

May R Lord JC hiself &God d Fatha Ncourage
yr harts &makeU strong in evry g%d deed
&word.
2 Thessalonians 2:16-17

*David and
Goliath.*

911 calls

Know someone who's having a hard time? Looking for something appropriate to send? Forget 'say it with flowers'... why not try saying it with words? Here are some words from the Bible already put into txt format, ready for you to send.

insecure about God?

Any1 who cums 2me I'll neva turn awa.
John 6:37

I'm confidnt th@ he who Bgan 2do g%d things in U wil keep on doin it til the Big Day of Gzus Xt.
Philippians 1:6

Theres no longa NE judgment on U, coz UR
in Xt Gzus.
Romans 8:1

If we walk in d lite (jus as he's in d lite) we
hav luv&peace w/each uva & d bl%d of Gzus
cleans awa all R sin.
1 John 1:7

Evry1 who receivs him, evry1 who blievs in
his name, is givn d rt 2 Bcum a child of God.
John 1:12

need 4giveness?

How hi is sky abuv erth? Th@'s how gr8
Gods luv is 4U. How far is E from W? Th@'s
how far yr sins hav been takn awa by God.
Psalm 103:11-12

If we fess R sins, he does wot he promisd:
he 4givs R sins & washes all R dirt clean.
1 John 1:9

4giv uvas their sins agenst U & God wil 4giv
yr sins agenst him.
Matthew 6:14

4giv uvas, jus as Gzus 4gave U.
Colossians 3:13

afraid?

Dont B afraid. Im yr shield, yr v gr8 reward.
Genesis 15:1

I searchd 4 da Lord &he heard me. He resQd
me from all my fears.
Psalm 34:4

Da Lord is my lite &my resQ: who shal I fear? Da Lord is d 4tress of my life: who wil make me afraid?
Psalm 27:1

I giv U my peace - not d world's version of peace, but mine. Dont let yr hearts B trubld & dont B afraid.
John 14:27

B strong, B ful of courage. Dont B afraid, dont B terrified. God goes w/U, God wil neva 4sake U.
Deuteronomy 31:6

Even tho I walk thru deth valley, I'll fear no evil, 4U R w/me.
Psalm 23:4

suffering?

Wot can separ8 us from Gods luv?
@ack?famine?danger?deth? No! Nuthin can
separ8 us from d luv of God in Gzus Xt.
Romans 8:35, 39

Da eternal God is yr refuge & underneath R
d everlasting arms.
Deuteronomy 33:27

Lets fix R eyes on Gzus, d beginning & end
of R faith, who 4 d joy set B4 him endurd d
X, scornd its shame & is now sitting @ d rt
h& of God.
Hebrews 12:2

Fear not. Ive redeemd U &calld U by name.
UR mine. If U pass thru d waters, Im w/U.

Go thru d rivas, they wont sweep U awa.
Walk thru d fire, U wont B burnd.
Isaiah 43:1-2

anxious?

Cum 2me, U who R tired &weighd down, & I
wil giv U rest. Take my yoke on U & lern
from me, 4 I am gentl & humbl &U wil find
rest 4 yr souls.
Matthew 11:28-29

Da peace of God, which can't B Xplaind or
undast%d, wil keep yr harts &minds in Xt
Gzus.
Philippians 4:7

Giv him all yr worries, Bcoz he cares 4U.
1 Peter 5:7

tempted?

Lead us not in2 temptation, but Dliver us
from d evil 1.
Matthew 6:13

Bcoz Gzus suffad when he was temptd, he
knows how to help us when we're temptd.
Hebrews 2:18

Yr NME d Devil prowls round lik a roaring
lion, hungry 2 eat sum1. B strong in yr faith
& resist him!
1 Peter 5:8-9

old
testmnt

d cre8un

It's one of the most famous passages in the Bible, read out by astronauts circling the moon on Christmas Day 1968. Here's the creation story, in various txt versions.

@1st, earf was nuffin.
day1:nite&day
day2:sky
day3:l&,c,@->
day4:sun,moon,*s
day5:<><,brds
day6:lnd animals,o{-<
God :o)
day7:rest
God zzzZZ
Genesis 1-2:4 (Sally Lewis, Uttoxeter, England)

Day1:lite;"cool"sed God.
2:sky;ditto.
3:earth+plants;ditto.
4:sun+moon+*s;ditto.
5:fish+birds;ditto.
6:animlz,ppl in his imaj;ditto.
7:God chilld.All good.
Genesis 1:1-2:3 (Susannah Cornwall, Exeter, England)

TBW G cre8d hvn&urth.
B4 tht urth ws a 4rmls 0,
H20 ws evrywhr; nyt ruled!
G ws thr 2, hufn&pufn.
G sd let der b lyt & voila!
G ws dlyted wid d lyt.
Genesis 1:1-4 (Nancy A. Carter, New York City, USA)

And now in pictures...

Day 1 - Light separated from darkness
_____ / @@@@

Day 2 - Waters parted to make sky
====== >8 ======

Day 3 - Waters gathered into one place
~~~~~//////

Day 4 - Stars, sun + moon
* * * / O / D

Day 5 - Fish + birds
<>< ^^ ^^ <><

Day 6 - Animals and man
U/=\~ O-|-<

Day 7 - God rested
Zzzzzzzzz

Genesis 1:1-2:3 (Paul W., Leeds, England)

1.Cre8 hvn,erth,day/nite-gd.

2.Sky-gd.

3.Land,C-gd.

4.Sun,moon,stars-gd.

5.Fish,birds-gd.

6.Beasts-gd.

M&F2rule.Cre8d lik God-vg.

7.Kip.

8.Snake,apel,Eve,uh,oh!

Genesis 1:1-2:3 and 3:1-24

(Andy Keulemans,
Wrexham, Wales)

10 com&ments

Read the original set of house rules for the human race, as chiselled in stone by Moses, in Exodus chapter 20. Below are 10 different txt versions, with the shortest (just 91 characters!) at the top.

jus me no uvas/no copiz/rspc mi nam/hona sunda & ur ma&pa/neva kil cht stl r lie/4get jelsi
(Nicola David, Ripon, England)

God: "Im No.1. No pix, plz. Uz my name nicely. Day7=holy. Take care of mum'n'dad. Dont kill, scrU round, steal or lie. Keep yr hands (&eyz) off wot isnt yrs!"
(Nick O'Demus, London, England)

The big10:God rulz4eva!Hav no other gods/ idols.Respec2his name,2Sunday(God made it)+2parents.Don't kill or cheat on ppl.Don't steal,slander or envy ppl's stuff.
(Susannah Cornwall, Exeter, England)

Da 10 dosNdonts: No god but god No idolz No cussng T8k a br8k on sunda Dont diss ma n pa No mrdr No sex b4 maridg Dont steal No lies Dont lust aftr ppl or stuff
(Warren Taylor, Cincinnati, OH, USA)

Im God, put me 1st. NEthing Ls wAsts time. No screw w/my nAm. SundAz 4U2 relX w/ me. No diss ya ma&pa. No kill,@ultry,stEl or lying bout ya nAba. Buy UR own stf
(Mark Butt, Hertford, England)

No uvaz no pix dont dis me respec sabbath mum and dad no kill no partner poachin no steal no lie no covet. No problem!
(Andy Keulemans, Wrexham, Wales)

do nt av ufer gds, do nt av idols, do nt dis my nm, onur ur rents, do nt kill, do nt b gilty of adultry, do nt steal, do nt lie, do nt covet, do nt wk sunday
(Lydia Bedford,
Guildford,
England)

the Lord=ur God, u will worship no others.
No idols or mistreating my name. Rest
Sunday. Honor parents. No killing/unmarried
sex/theft/lying/coveting.
(Clarke Rice, Coleraine, N. Ireland)

U shl Luv God only, No IdolRtrE, honR his
nAm, keep sabRth Oly, honR dad & mum, U
shl not mrdr, nor cmit adltRE, nor stEl, nor
lI, nor DsIR sum 1 Lses stuf,
(Stephen Leeke, Cambridge, England)

I'm God, no otha. Wow nowt else or 2b trbl!
Diss not my nm, Ih8 it. Holyday 1/7. Rspk
yo ma&pa. Kill not. No 4nic8n. Nik nowt. No
porkies. :'s off pals' stuff!
(Andrew Duff, London, England)

psalms

The Psalms... where the Bible breaks into song. Here are 22 extracts from the song lyrics of the Bible. If you're looking for Psalm 23, turn to page 78.

In peace I lie down&sleep,
coz u Lord make me dwell in safety.
Psalm 4:8

God,brilnt lrd.
evry1 nos ur name.
nursin infnts gurgle bout u.
todlers shout songs,
drown out NME babble.
i look@ur skies&marvel.
ur name echoes rnd the wrld.
Psalm 8 (Claire Hollywell, Horsham, England)

Da f%l sez in his heart: "God=0".
Psalm 14:1

May my mouth speak
&my heart think
in a way th@ pleases U,
O Lord, my rock'n'redeemer.
Psalm 19:14

T8st & C dat d Lord is good!
Psalm 34:8

I w8d patiently 4 d Lord
& he herd my cry.
Liftd me outa d mud&mire.
Put my feet ona rock.
Gave me a nu song of prayz to my God.
Psalm 40:1-3

God's R refuge&strenf,
helping when we're in trubl 24/7.
There4 we wont fear,
evn tho d erth crumbls
& whole mts fall in2 d C.
Psalm 46:1-2

B still & no I m Gd
Psalm 46:10 (Dalwyn Attwell, Windsor,
England)

Cre8 in me a nu heart O Lrd
& renu a rite Sprt in me.
Psalm 51:10 (Dalwyn Attwell, Windsor,
England)

God alone is my rok & my salvatn.
He is my 4tress, I wil neva B shaken.
Psalm 62:2

Lets bow down in worship,
lets neel B4 d Lord R maker,
4 heez R God & we R d ppl of his pasture,
d flock unda his care.
Psalm 95:6-7

Rayz th ruf4God!
Wrk4HmNgladns&sing!
HzRLord!
We cudnt makus - He had2!
Wer lamz on Hz farm.
Go N2 hz gatz N thnx&praz.
Bles hz name!
Hez gud,mercifl&tru4eva!
Psalm 100 (Loretta Nile, Raleigh, NC, USA)

Mk a joyfl noiz n2 th Lrd, L ye lnds!
Psalm 100:1 (Andy B., Alpha, IL, USA)

Da Lord=God.
He made us & we R his.
We R his ppl,
d sheep of his pasture.
So Nter his g8s wiv tx
& his courts wiv prayz.
Giv tx 2him & prayz his name.
Psalm 100:3-4

The original text message
(Daniel 5:25)

Say tx 2 God, 4 he is gd,
his luv goes on 4 eva.
Psalm 107:1 (LOAF, Bristol, England)

Happy is person who oners God,
who Njoys obeying his laws.
Psalm 112:1 (LOAF, Bristol, England)

Frm the east 2 the west,
praise the name of God.
Psalm 113:3 (LOAF, Bristol, England)

2day's "Made by God". Rejoice! B glad!
Psalm 118:24

Yr word is a lamp 4my feet, a lite 4my path.
Psalm 119:105

God u ave looked @ me + u no me.
U no wen I sit + wen I rise.
U no wot I fink.
U no all I do.
B4 a word is on my tong U no it God.
Psalm 139:1-4 (LOAF, Bristol, England)

Evry day i'll say tx,
i'll praise u 4eva +eva.
Psalm 145:2 (LOAF, Bristol, England)

A10shun evrything that breathes:
prayz d Lord!
Psalm 150:6

d Lord z my shepud

The world-famous Psalm 23, written by David, shepherd-turned-king...

GuidinGod loox out4me,
takin me2safe places+givin peace.
He keeps me rt+protex me
evn nr death+evl.
My NMEs just look on.
Wen God's there,gdness+mercy R2,
4eva.
(Susannah Cornwall, Exeter, England)

God watches me,
keeps me calm,
tells me 2 go.
Not scared 4UR ere.
U feed me + fill me.
U luv me 4eva.
(Peter Sterling, Barnsley, England)

Gods my sheped, I wont want.
I ly in gras&sit@stil H2Os.
E gvs me strenf&gides my pafs.
I wont fear cos u protect me.
U bles me&fil my cup.
Ur luvs wiv me 4eva.
(Joy B., Stoke-on-Trent, England)

4 evrything theres a Czun

Turned into the pop hit 'Turn! Turn! Turn!' by The Byrds in 1965, but written approx. 2,200 years before that, the words of Ecclesiastes chapter 3 are something special. Here are two versions.

4 evrythng theres a Czun.
Time 2B born &2 die.
2weep & 2laff.
2morn & 2dance.
2keep & 2chuck.
2shut it & 2talk.
2luv & 2h8.
Time 4war & 4peace.

thrza tym 4
FRE prpS Ndr hvn
2Bbrn&2dy
2so&2reap
2kil&2heal
2cry&2laf
2morn&2jig
2hug&2not
2win&2luz
2kep&2tos
2rip&2so
2hsh&2tlk
2luv&2h@e
4war&4peas
Ecclesiastes 3:1-8 (Tim Stoughton,
Sioux City, IA, USA)

gr8 OT txts

If any one part of the Bible was just made for text messaging, it's the book of Proverbs, which has chapter after chapter of smart two-liners, just the right length for keying in. There are lots of proverbs here, plus other memorable bits of the Old Testament.

Go 2 it 2 do it!
Genesis 1:28 (Andy B., Alpha,
Illinois, USA)

N da bgning god cr8td all n 6 daz. On da 7th day he chilld.
Genesis 1:1, 2:2 (Warren Taylor,
Cincinnati, OH, USA)

Noah tuk hs famli &anmls 2bi2 in2 de ark.God fluded urf& ark woz @ sea 4 4e days.Afta vry1 else died God sed 2Noah I prmse neva 2flud urf agen& dis rnbo sez so. *Genesis 7:7–9:13 (Nicola David, Ripon, England)*

snk smrt.
snk:Ueat0?
ev:all but1tree.
snk:Y?
ev:dy.
snk:no!UC!
ev8.adm2.
Gd:wearRU?Ueat?
adm:blam ev!
ev:blam snk!
Gd:URbad!
snk eat dst!
ev BB hurt!
adm wrk!
Genesis 3:1-23 (Tim Stoughton, Sioux City, IA, USA)

Go 4th + x
Genesis 9:7 (Andrew Blyth, Luton, England)

God iz my protection ware-eva i go.
Genesis 28:15 (Lydia Bedford, Guildford, England)

i 4 i, 2th 4 2th, h& 4 h&, fut 4 fut.
Exodus 21:24 (Colleen P. Arndt, Medford, OR, USA)

let God bless+look afta u
let God :) + b gracious 2 u
let God giv u P's
Numbers 6:24-26 (Catherine Jones, Sunderland, England)

Dis cmandmnt not hidn, not n hevn (who gonna fly der?) or byond C (who swim?) but n ur hearts. Life/deth, gd/evil, blesng/curse: ur pick, but God recmends life.
Deuteronomy 30:11-19 (Vince, Taipei, Taiwan)

B strong. Try ur very best. Obey all laws. Not
turn frm laws to left or rite. Then u'll ave
success woteva u do.
Joshua 1:7-8 (LOAF, Bristol, England)

Be strong &brave cos I am the Lord &I am
with U evrywhere.
Joshua 1:7, 9 (Clarke Rice, Coleraine,
N. Ireland)

O God bles me. Giv me more of ur work.
Let ur hand b wiv me. Keep me safe.
Keep me free frm pain.
1 Chronicles 4:9-10 (LOAF, Bristol, England)

Trust in the Lord wiv all yr hart, &lean not
un2 yr own understanin. In all yr ways
aknowledge him & he'll direct yr paths.
Proverbs 3:5-6 (Gary Hall, Liverpool, England)

And now... the whole Bible
in one txt msg

Cre8 all.
Sin.
Deth.
Promise Abe kids.
Egypt,Red C,desert.
Israel.
More sin.
Exile.
Hope.
JC-God incarn8.
Luvd,h8d,cross,ded.
Rises>hvn.
HS,Ch,JC2 rtn & win!

(Andy Keulemans, Wrexham, Wales)

If U gather crops in da summa, U'll eat.
If U sleep thru da harvest, well, duh!
Proverbs 10:5

Pride can only lead U2 disgrace.
But humility wil makeU Yz.
Proverbs 11:2

The fool is 100% sure he's on the rt rd,
but Yz ppl ask uvaz 4 advice.
Proverbs 12:15

The f%l gets angry in 2secs,
but the Yz person ignores an insult.
Proverbs 12:16

Yz ppl kno how 2 keep schtum,
but f%ls blab their idioC.
Proverbs 12:23

There's a road that l%ks c%l,
but its d road 2 deth.
Proverbs 14:12

Evn wen yr laffing,
yr heart can ache.
Proverbs 14:13

If u want 2 stay out of trble,
B careful wot u say.
Proverbs 21:23 (LOAF, Bristol, England)

3 things R 2 amazing:
bird in sky
snake on rock
ship on C
way of man n woman.
Proverbs 30:18-19 (Ryan Cordell, Kandern, Germany)

Gd wife: who can find 1?
AbleBabe,Can,Duz.Erly Fud Giver.Holy In2
Jah.Knits.Lamp Must Not Out.Purple
Quilts.Rich.Spins.Talents.UnaVailable.Wise,Xtra
Ys.Zealous.
*Proverbs 31 (Andy Keulemans, Wrexham,
Wales)*

It's best 2 ave wise ppl scold U
than ave dumb ppl
sing ur praises.
*Ecclesiastes 7:5
(LOAF, Bristol,
England)*

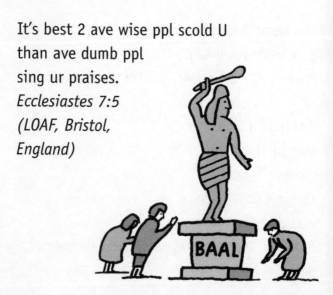

My beautiful darlng:
U I's R birds
U teeth like white sheep
U lips R red ribbon
U temple like fruit
U breasts R like fawns
UR beautiful N perfect.
Song of Songs 4:1-7 (Ryan Cordell,
Kandern, Germany)

U rich n powrfl, im bootifl.Cmon lie w/me,
kiss my black body,its natrl.Solomon:woo-
wee,bzms like twin gazelles,im sold!(This
symboliz Xt/church relatnshp.)
Song of Songs (Vince, Taipei, Taiwan)

God gvs > pwr 2 the wEk
yet the yng tire,trip&fall.
But 1 who trsts God gets strengf
2 wlk,run & even fly hi.
Isaiah 40:29-31 (Mark P. Sanford,
Folkestone, England)

Dey dat w8 on de Lord shal renu der strengf,
dey shal mt up wiv wings as eagles, dey shal
run &not B weri, dey shal walk &not faint.
Isaiah 40:31 (Gary Hall, Liverpool, England)

God, I no tht no1 is the msta of his own
destiny; no1 controls his own life.
Jeremiah 10:23 (LOAF, Bristol, England)

B lke a tree plnted by H20 tht spreds its
roots 2 the rvr. Whn drght cmes U wll bear
fruit.
*Jeremiah 17:8 (Dana Bogany, Pittsburgh,
PA, USA)*

I no wot I plan 4U says God.
I've gd plans 4U not 2 hurt U.
I'll giv U hope + a gd life.
Jeremiah 29:11 (LOAF, Bristol, England)

God sez: "I no wot I hav 4U. Stuf 2 prosper
U, not 2 harm U, 2 giv U hope & a future."
*Jeremiah 29:11 (Andy, Campbell, London,
England)*

nu
testmnt

da word

'In the beginning was the Word...' The opening verses of John chapter 1 are turned into txt...

Wd was 1st. Wd was God. Wd cre8ed all.
John 1:1-3 (Mary Hawkins, Tavistock, England)

B4 NEthin was the wrd.the wrd was wiv god
& was god. Nufin was made wivout him.
Life-lite blazed outa darknes and nufin
could put it out.
John 1:1-5 (Claire Hollywell, Horsham, England)

Word@start, with God, was God.
John 1:1 (Amanda Stevens, Birmingham, England)

In da beginning woz da wrd. Da wrd woz wiv God & da wrd woz God.

John 1:1 (Matthew Watts, London, England)

N the bgnning was the wrd & the wrd was wth Gd, & the wrd was Gd.

John 1:1 (Dana Bogany, Pittsburgh, PA, USA)

1st: Word; Word & God; Word = God.

John 1:1 (Dalwyn Attwell, Windsor, England)

The first mobile phone.

4 gospels

If you're looking for Jesus' most striking words, look no more. Here they are. Together with some of the stories from Matthew, Mark, Luke and John.

In mth6 Gd snt NJL2Mary.
NJL:hi!Gd w/U,luckEU!
Mry:huh?
NJL:fear0,URspshl2Gd &UR2havaBB2calGsus.
he2rain4FR.
Mry:how?
NJL:holygst. 4w/Gd0impsbl.
Mry:OK.
NJL:by!
*Luke 1:26-38 (Tim Stoughton,
Sioux City, IA, USA)*

Aleluja! Gd has an I on me. Evry1 sez Im
blesd cos da Bos is gd 2me. Fear im &E is
gr8 - E srted da badguys & gve grub 2 da
MT. E has bin fab 2us - E sed E wud.
Mary's Song in Luke 1:46-55 (Janice Fixter,
Croydon, England)

Lord letme go nPeace,
azU sed.
IC baby=Usavus.
U plandit 4all2C.
Lite 4goyim!
Glory 4juz!
Simeon's Song in Luke 2:29-32 (Arthur
French, Ipplepen, Devon, England)

John wor camlhair clothes wiva levabelt &he 8locusts &honey &e sed Aftr me wil com1 mor powrful than I. I bptize wiv watr he wil bptize wiv Holy Spirit.
Mark 1:6-8 (Seb Apostol, Leamington, England)

By thC JC saw Simon &broAndrew castng nets in2th lake 4they wer fishrs Cum folo me JCsed &Ill makQ fishrsofmen they lft thr nets &folod him.
Mark 1:16-18 (Seb Apostol, Leamington, England)

Its not helthy ppl who need a Dr, but d sick. I havent cum 4 d ppl who think theyre OK, but 4 sinnas.
Mark 2:17

No 1 can C d kingdm of God unless they R born again.
John 3:3

Nicodemus go2 Jesus @night &say: "UR of God." Jesus: "U must B born again." Nic: "huh?" Jesus: "God loved &gave Son 4world so U can B 4given &live 4ever."
John 3:1-21 (Clarke Rice, Coleraine, N. Ireland)

Lite has cum in2 d world, but ppl luvd d dark insted of d lite, coz their deeds wer evil.
John 3:19

If U drink d water I giv U, U'll neva B thirsty. It'll Bcum a spring inside U, givin U eternal life.
John 4:14

:-) R de pure @ <3 4 dey shal C G*D
Matthew 5:8 (Ken Brown, London, England)

UR d salt of d erth. Dont lose yr salty flava,
or U'll be g%d 4 nuthin!
Matthew 5:13

Let me tel U Y UR here: 2B salt & bring out
god flavours of the earth. 2B light and show
the world its true god colours.
We're goin public wiv
this - shine!
Matthew 5:13-15
(Claire Hollywell,
Horsham, England)

Jesus calls the 12 disciples.

UR d lite of d world. Let yr lite shine B4 evry1 so they can see how U live & prayz yr Fathr in hvn.
Matthew 5:14-16

Dont swear. Let yr yes=yes & yr no=no.
Matthew 5:34, 37

U hear I4I. I say no resist evil man. If hit, turn 4 another. If take tunic, giv cloak. If forced 1 mile, go 2. Giv 2 1 who asks. No turn from 1 who borrows.
Matthew 5:38-42 (Ryan Cordell, Kandern, Germany)

If NE1 hits d RH side of yr face, turn d LH side 4 them 2 hit as wel. If NE1 4ces U 2 walk 1 mile, go 2 miles w/them.
Matthew 5:39, 41

Dont judge &U wont B judgd. Dont condem &U wont B condemd. 4giv &U will B 4givn.
Luke 6:37

Luv yr NMEs & pray 4those who perCQt U so U may B childrn of yr Fathr in hvn.
Matthew 5:44-45

Luv ur NMEs, pray 4 thse hu curse U. If 1 slps U on da cheek offa da otha 1. Treat ppl as U wud like 2B treatd. By doin dis U'll rcv a gr8 rewrd in hevn.
Luke 6:27-35 (Sharleen Nall-Evans, Cheshire, England)

Y look @ d tiny speck in sum1 else's eye when there's a gr8 big plank in yr own?
Luke 6:41

Dont worry bout yr life. L%k @ d birds! They dont do NE farming or shopping, yet yr hvnly Fathr feeds em.
Matthew 6:25-26

Dont worry bout 2morro, 4 2morro wil worry bout itself.
Matthew 6:34

Wan2 save yr life? U'll lose it! But if U lose yr life 4 my sake, U'll save it.
Mark 8:35

Ask! It'll B givn. Seek! U'll find. Knock knock! "It's open!"
Matthew 7:7

"Permission to land, sir..."

Wot g%d is it if U win d whole world but l%se yr soul?
Mark 8:36

Do 2 uthers wat U want em 2 do 2U. Dis is da meanin of da law of our m8 Moses n da uther teachers.
Matthew 7:12 (Lydia Bedford, Guildford, England)

B2 uvas wot U want them 2B2U
Matthew 7:12 (Philip Law, Harrow, England)

Do 4 ppl wot U wud like em 2do 4U.
Matthew 7:12 (Catherine Jones, Sunderland, England)

Str8 is d g8 & narro is d way th@ leads 2life, & few there B th@ find it.
Matthew 7:14

5 loaves + 2<>< + thnx = food 4 5000 + 12 baskets full.
John 6:1-14 (Sally Lewis, Uttoxeter, Staffordshire, England)

I'm d lite of d world. Follo me & U'll neva walk in darknss, but wil hav d lite of life.
John 8:12

A storm broke ova da lake & Jesus was zzz. Dscpls wer scard &woke him. He sed: "Y RU scared? Av u no faif?" He calmd da lake &they wer amazd @ him.
Matthew 8:23-27 (Sharleen Nall-Evans, Cheshire, England)

Its a big harvest, but theres hardly NE1 2 work @ bringing it in. Ask d Lord of d harvest, there4, 2 send a load mo workers.
Matthew 9:37-38

Im sending U out lik sheep among wolves. So B as Yz as snakes & innocent as duvs.
Matthew 10:16

Do U wan2B w/me? Deny yrself, take up yr X & follo me.
Mark 8:34

Jsus told em anuther story: "My place is lyk a mustard seed, da seed iz small but growz 2B v-big, big enuf 4birds 2nest in."
Matthew 13:31-32 (Lydia Bedford, Guildford, England)

Gsus sent out 72 discples in 2s. "Wear 0 shoes, stA in 1 house, hl the sick, say the kgdm is nr."
Luke 10:1-9 (Mary Hawkins, Tavistock, England)

Sparrows are 5 4 2pence. Yet not evn 1 sparrow is 4gotn by God. Evry hair on yr head is numbrd: 1,2,3,etc... So dont B afraid. UR worth more than d sparrows.
Luke 12:6-7

U must B ready. Da son of man wil cum @ an hour when U dont Xpect him.
Luke 12:40

Xalt yrself & U'll B humbld. & vysaversa.
Luke 14:11

Hvn throws a bigger party ova 1 sinna who repents than ova 99 holy ppl who dont need 2 repent!
Luke 15:7

U cant serve 2 bosses. Eitha U'll h8 No.1 & luv No.2, or B Dvoted 2 No.1 & Dspise No.2. U can't serve God & $$$.
Luke 16:13

Even w/faith as small as a mustard seed, U can tell a mountain: "Move it!" & it'll obey!
Matthew 17:20

Da kingdm of God is within U.
Luke 17:21

Bcum like a little child, or U'll neva enta d kingdm of hvn.
Matthew 18:3

I'm d g8. Enter thru me & U'll B savd. U'll be free to cum in & go out & find pasture.
John 10:9

Where 2or3 get 2getha in my name, I'm rt there w/them.
Matthew 18:20

"How many times shd I 4give uvaz?" askd
Peter. "7x?" "No!" sed Gzus. "70x7!"
Matthew 18:21-22

I came so U mite av life 2 da max.
John 10:10 (Stephanie, Belfast, N. Ireland)

It's EZer 4 a camel 2go thru d eye of a
needle than 4 a richman 2 get in2 d kingdm
of God!
Mark 10:25

Da 1st willB last & da last willB 1st.
Mark 10:31

j:.(
*John 11:35 (Richard Smeltzer, Hamilton,
Ontario, Canada)*

Jesus ;(
John 11:35 (Richard Koppinger, Summit, NJ, USA)

Didnt I say dat if U blieved U wud C da glory of our gr8 God?
John 11:40 (Lydia Bedford, Guildford, England)

Hvn&erth wil pass awa, but my words are 4ever.
Luke 21:33

Now dat I ur buddy av washed ur feet U shod go also and wash 1 n-uthers feet.
John 13:14 (Lydia Bedford, Guildford, England)

Ive set U an xample: dat U shud do as Ive dun 4U.
John 13:14 (Lydia Bedford, Guildford, England)

I'm d vine. UR d branches. Stay plugd in & U'll produce a loada fruit. Get unplugd & U'll dry up. Apart from me, U can do 0.
John 15:5

Luv each uva as I've luvd U.
John 15:12

@ noon, Pil8 sed: "Here is Ur kg." They sed: "Put him on a X. We hav 0 kg but Caesr." So Pil8 gav Gsus 2 them 2B put on a X.
John 19:14-16 (Mary Hawkins, Tavistock, England)

11 go up mt. Worship Jsus. Some doubt. Jsus says: "All powr is givn me. Go make discples evrywhere. Baptize in God, Son, Spirit. Teach them. I with U always.
Matthew 28:20 (Ryan Cordell, Kandern, Germany)

I wil B with U 24/7, 2 d end of time.
Matthew 28:20

There4 go n make disciples of all da nations, baptise em in da nm of da Big Guy n of da Son n da Oly Spirit!
Matthew 28:19 (Lydia Bedford, Guildford, England)

d beatitudes

**Starting with 'blessed are the poor...'
Jesus gives one of the best-known
passages of the Bible. These txt versions
of the Beatitudes sadly don't include
Monty Python's 'blessed are the
cheesemakers...'**

Hpy RU por; da kngdm is yrs!
Hpy RU hngry; U wl Bfild!
Hpy RU sad; u wl lol!
Hpy RU whn ppl h8 U Bcos of da Lrd!
B gld&dnce 4jy Bcos a gt prz is kpt 4U in
hvn.
*Luke 6:20-23 (Hannah,
Welwyn Garden City, England)*

Ur blesd when uv lost it al,
gods kgdom's ther 2find!
Ur blesd when ur hungry,
ur ready 2eat mesianic food.
Ur blesd when tears flo,
joy comes in the morn.
*Luke 6:20-21 (Claire Hollywell,
Horsham, England)*

God's will: Poor n Oprest get whl hvnly
shebang 2 shr w/peacemakers. Mourners gt
cum4t. Meek gt Earth. Justice-hankerers gt
it. Mercy 4merciful. Pure gt 2C God.
*Matthew 5:3-9 (Libby Hudson,
Herefordshire, England)*

R4thr URN hvn

**'Pop on high...' 'RBoss in hvn...' and
'Divine Dad...' are just three ways to turn
the Lord's Prayer into txt. Here are 10
versions of the prayer – choose the one
you like best.**

dad@hvn,ur spshl.
we want wot u want
&urth2b like hvn.
giv us food&4giv r sins
lyk we 4giv uvaz.
don't test us!save us!
bcos we kno ur boss,
ur tuf&ur cool
4 eva!ok?
(Matthew Cambell, York, England)

r pa in evan, respect 2u,
may u rain ear as in evan.
giv us r needs,
4giv r sin as we 4giv r nmes.
resq us from the evil 1.
4 ur always the most xlent dude.
yo
(Steve Seymour, Bristol, England)

God@heaven.org,
You rule, up and down.
We need grub and a break.
Will pass it on.
Keep us focused.
You totally rule, long term.
Amen.
(Stephen E. Moore, Bellevue, WA, USA)

Hi Fr., Mat 6:9-13 again pls. Cheers. c u in ch.
(Andy Keulemans, Wrexham, Wales)

R4thr URN hvn
Bigup2U
Yo kngdm cm
Do ur wil on rth azN hvn
Givz2day Rdayz bred
N4giv Rsinz
We 4giv RNMEz
No tmptng plz
Savuz frm evl
4UR wkd&amzng
4eva(x2)MN!
(Naomi, Leeds, England)

Fthr@hvn.hlwd b u,
ur kndm cum ur wil b dun,
@ rth as in hvn.
Giz 2d r dly brd,
4giv r sins z we 4giv othrs.
Led us nt in2 tptn
Bt dlvr us frm evl.
4eva amen!
(Seb Apostol, Leamington, England)

RBoss in hvn yr name rocks.
Yr rules rule.
Give us food.
Give us breaks.
We'll give others breaks 2.
We're weak.
Keep us fr bad stuff.
Bc all is yrs 4ever. Amen
(Catherine, Purchase, NY, USA)

Pop on high, cool name,
rule!win!here too.
give & forgive-cuz we do.
save us for your pad,
power & glory - always.
chow
(Ed, Lincoln, England)

Divine Dad,
Holy is yo name+realm.
Doing here = as in heaven.
Ur our provider,
4give us as we 4give others.
Save us from Satan.
U da king & all that 4ever.
Bye
(Lawrence Lapointe, Houston, TX, USA)

Hi God UR gr8
what U want OK.
Feed us 4give us
4 we 4give.
Don't tempt, save.
All is 4U always
Amen
(Howard Langmead, Melbourne, Australia)

R Fthr, UR holy.
B with us
so Ur will B done as in hvn.
Give what we need
+ 4give us - we 4give ppl.
Turn us from sin + evil.
4 all Blongs 2U 4evr.
Amen.
(Colin Jenkins, Glasgow, Scotland)

RFather in hevn,
Holy b yr name
B king&hav yr way in earth as hevn
Giv us food 4 2day
4giv us as we 4giv
Keep us from trial&evil
U reign in powr&glory 4ever
OK!
(Jessica Percival, Enfield, England)

John 3:16

How do you turn the Bible's e=mc² into sms? Here's how...

God luvd world. His son died 4it. Blieve in him &B saved.

god luvd the wrld so much th@ he gave his 1&only son.y?so no1 gets dstryd but if they belive,can have evalastin life.
(Claire Hollywell, Horsham, England)

Gd lvd, Gd gave, U blv, U'r svd!
(Andy B., Alpha, IL, USA)

4 Gd lvd us so, he snt his nly sn 4 us 2 liv 4eva & nt di. Nt snt 2 juj bt 2 save us.
(Neil Jackson, Wakefield, England)

I am...

The seven 'I am' sayings of Jesus, taken from John's Gospel...

I'm d bred of life. *(John 6:35)*

I'm d lite of d world. *(John 8:12)*

I'm d g8 4 d sheep. *(John 10:7)*

I'm d g%d shepud. *(John 10:11)*

I'm d resurexn &d life. *(John 11:25)*

I'm d way, truf & life. *(John 14:6)*

I'm d tru vine. *(John 15:1)*

ρistles frm
d ρostles

Ever been tempted to read other people's mail? That's what you're doing if you read the back end of the New Testament. These letters to the first Christians are full of good stuff... and they're now available in txt.

If God is 4 us who can B against us?
Romans 8:31 (Matthew Watts, London, England)

Wot sepr8s us frm Jesus: tuf stuff? No, we R winaz ova all& 4eva cos he luvs us. 0 gd r bad can sepr8 us frm Godz luv in him.
Romans 8:35-39 (Nicola David, Ripon, England)

Nthing can sepR8 uz frm Gds lv. Dth cant & lfe cant, angls cant & dmns cant. Worries 4 2day & 2mrO cant - evn da powZ of hll cant kp hz love away.

Romans 8:38-39 (Gordon Rouse, Cambridge, England)

Wot can separ8 us frm Gods luv? @ack?famine?danger?deth? No! Nothing can separ8 us frm d luv of God in Gzus Xt.

Romans 8:35, 39

Scrolling through your messages in ancient times.

B Dvoted 2 1annuva in luv
Romans 12:10 (Philip Law, Harrow, England)

Greet 1 nuther wiv a holy :-*
2 Corinthians 13:12

Grace LJC, Luv God, FLOship HS B wth U all.
2 Corinthians 13:14 (Dalwyn Attwell,
Windsor, England)

Now 2him who can do 1000x more than we
eva ask&imagine, acc/2 his powr @work in
us, 2him B glory in d chrch & in Xt Gzus, 4
eva&eva! Rmen.
Ephesians 3:20-21

B not %-) w/wine. Insted B filld w/da Spirit.
Ephesians 5:18

Gods powrs lyk armor 2keepU strong frm evl.
Wear it: belt4truth, brestpl8 4right,
shoes4peace, shield4faith, helmt4savin. His
word is spirichl sword. Uzit&pray.
Ephesians 6:10-18 (Susannah Cornwall,
Exeter, England)

If Uv got NEthin from folowin Chrst, if
Ucare, do me a favr, agre wiv each ova, luv
each ova, B deep spiritd frends. 4get urselvs
long enuf 2lend a helpin hand.
Philippians 2:1-2 (Claire Hollywell, Horsham,
England)

Hve a 'tude like JC.
Philippians 2:5 (Dana Bogany, Pittsburgh,
PA, USA)

Rejoice in d Lord 24/7! Say it wiv me: Rejoice!
Philippians 4:4

Repeat prasin Gd. B gentle 2 all: Gd's nr. Dont fear, always ask Gd n C Gd's way-out peace. 40fy ur harts n minds in Gsus.
Philippians 4:4-7 (Matthew Button, Leeds, England)

B hppy in God alwys. Yes B hppy. Let every1 C ur gentlnes. God is close.
Philippians 4:4-5 (LOAF, Bristol, England)

Dont B worried bout anyfing but pray bout everyfing. Say tx &ask God 4wot U need.
Philippians 4:6 (LOAF, Bristol, England)

Woteva is noble, rite, pure&luvly, if anyfing
is fab or due praise, fink bout such fings.
Philippians 4:8 (LOAF, Bristol, England)

UR childrn of lite+day. We don't Blong 2
nite or dark. So B awake & B self-controld.
*1 Thessalonians 5:5-6 (LOAF, Bristol,
England)*

Txt-heckling.

Hlp ppl who R scared. Hlp ppl who R weak.
B patient wiv every1.
1 Thessalonians 5:14 (LOAF, Bristol, England)

B sure no1 finks 2 rongs make a right. Alwys
try 2 do wot is gd 4 uvas + 4 all ppl.
1 Thessalonians 5:15 (LOAF, Bristol, England)

Test all fings. Keep the gd stuf. Stay away
frm all the evil stuf.
*1 Thessalonians 5:21-22 (LOAF, Bristol,
England)*

Say hi to uvas wiv a holy hug.
1 Thessalonians 5:26 (LOAF, Bristol, England)

Grace of Jsus B wiv U.
1Thessalonians 5:28 (LOAF, Bristol, England)

Gzus Crst is da same ysterda n 2day n 4evr.
Hebrews 13:8 (Matthew Coker, Clovis,
NM, USA)

Jsus is same yestrday, 2day & 4evamore.
Hebrews 13:8 (LOAF, Bristol, England)

JC roolz! Yesterday, 2day & 4eva!
Hebrews 13:8 (Matthew Watts, London,
England)

JC: the same yestrday, 2day & 4 eva.
Hebrews 13:8

UR of God, litl children, &hav overcum evil,
4 gr8ter is he dat is in U dan he dat is in
the world.
1 John 4:4 (Gary Hall, Liverpool, England)

Dr Frndz, letz luv 1another coz luv cums frm God.
1 John 4:7 (Janet & Dave Parkins,
Huddersfield, England)

2him hu keepsU frm fallin &will prsnt
UB4his glrius presns w/o falt&w/gr8 joy,
2the1God RSavior Bglry,mjsty,pwr&athoriT
thru JCRLord,B4all ages, now&4FRmor,Amn!
Jude 24-25 (Tim Stoughton, Sioux City,
IA, USA)

I am A&Z, 1st & Lst. I is, was, willB. D
gr8tst!
Revelation 1:8 (Dalwyn Attwell, Slough,
England)

d gr8est
is luv

It's a short chapter, 1 Corinthians 13, but a bit too long to fit into one txt msg. So here are some extracts from one of St Paul's most inspiring moments...

Luv's more than clevr talk.
It's kind,gentl,meek,strong,
4givin,true+faithfl.
It endures more than all.
Kids' ways+darknss end.
Faith+hope go on;luv is 4eva.
1 Corinthians 13 (Susannah Cornwall, Exeter,
England)

Tho i spEk da lingo of 0:-)s
if ive no luv im a boomn gong.
i cud av da faif 2 move a mt
but wivout luv im nothn.
3 remain: faif hope & luv.
& da gr8st is luv.
1 Corinthians 13:1, 2, 13 (Sharleen Nall-
Evans, Cheshire, England)

Luv waits, is kind, no NV, not proud.
Not rude or self-seekin, no quick
anger. Not HapP w/evil -
hapP w/truth. 4ever
protects, trusts, hopes.
Luv fails not.
1 Corinthians 13:4-8
(Ryan Cordell,
Kandern, Germany)

Amen.

d dead C txts: ansas

Answers to the dead C txts on page 47:

1. B^(---> 8^)
The blind man sees (John 9:25).

2. E:8) x1000 ---> H20
The Gadarene swine plunge over a cliff into the Sea of Galilee (Mark 5:13).

3.]:-)]:-)]:-) —> *
The three kings follow the star (Matthew 2:9).

4.]:$) .... :=81
King Solomon is thrilled with his new baboon on a chain (1 Kings 10:22).

5. &(:-)## ----<o><
Peter catches a fish with a coin inside it
(Matthew 17:27).

6.):-(### o---- ---> ~~~~o<
Aaron's stick turns into a snake
(Exodus 7:10).

7. <>(:-) ---> (:-P
The day of Pentecost, with flames on heads
and speaking in tongues (Acts 2:3-4).

8. _i_/ ---> ><i >
Jonah quits the boat and ends up inside a
fish (Jonah 1:15-17).

9. #(:-)## ---> 8>< ---> (:-(
Samson gets a fatal haircut (Judges 16:19).

10. 00000 <>< <><

Jesus' miracle of five loaves and two fish
(Luke 9:16).

11. _____iiiiii_____////

The Israelites cross the Red Sea
(Exodus 14:21-22).

12. ////eeeee

The Egyptians terminally fail to cross the
Red Sea (Exodus 14:27-28).

thanx

Thanks to everyone who contributed txt msgs to this book by responding to the competition on ship-of-fools.com. All contributors are credited next to their individual msgs, except for the pictograms in d nu hieroglyphix (page 18) and d dead C txts (page 47), due to reasons of space. So here they are.

Contributors to d nu hieroglyphix are: Steve Tomkins of London, England, for church, synagogue, church of Satan, David dancing before the Lord, John Wesley. The Coot of Perth, Australia, for Calvary (horizontal), Lot's wife, the Gadarene demoniac and swine, and the Catholic bishop. Marmot for the Spirit descends as a dove, dove brings olive branch to Noah, and the Evil One. Maureen Hastings of New Hampshire, USA, for the grim reaper and gluttony. Philip Law of Harrow, England, for Jacob's dream and Diana, goddess of the Ephesians. Andrea Sparrow of Windsor, England, for Samson (pre-haircut).

Contributors to d dead C txts are: The Coot (1). Steve Tomkins (10). Andrea Sparrow (11). Carys Underdown of Cambridge, England (12).

All uncredited txts in this book are by Simon Jenkins.

Ship-of-fools.com is the irreverent, satirical (and sometimes ridiculously funny) internet magazine and online community.

Subtitled 'the magazine of Christian unrest', the ship is famous for its discussion boards, including Heaven, Hell, Purgatory and Dead Horses. 'They make other Christian bulletin boards look anaemic,' says the *Church Times*.

Visit, read, lurk and join ship-of-fools.com!